THIS COLORING BOOK
BELONGS TO:

ISBN: 9798673900215

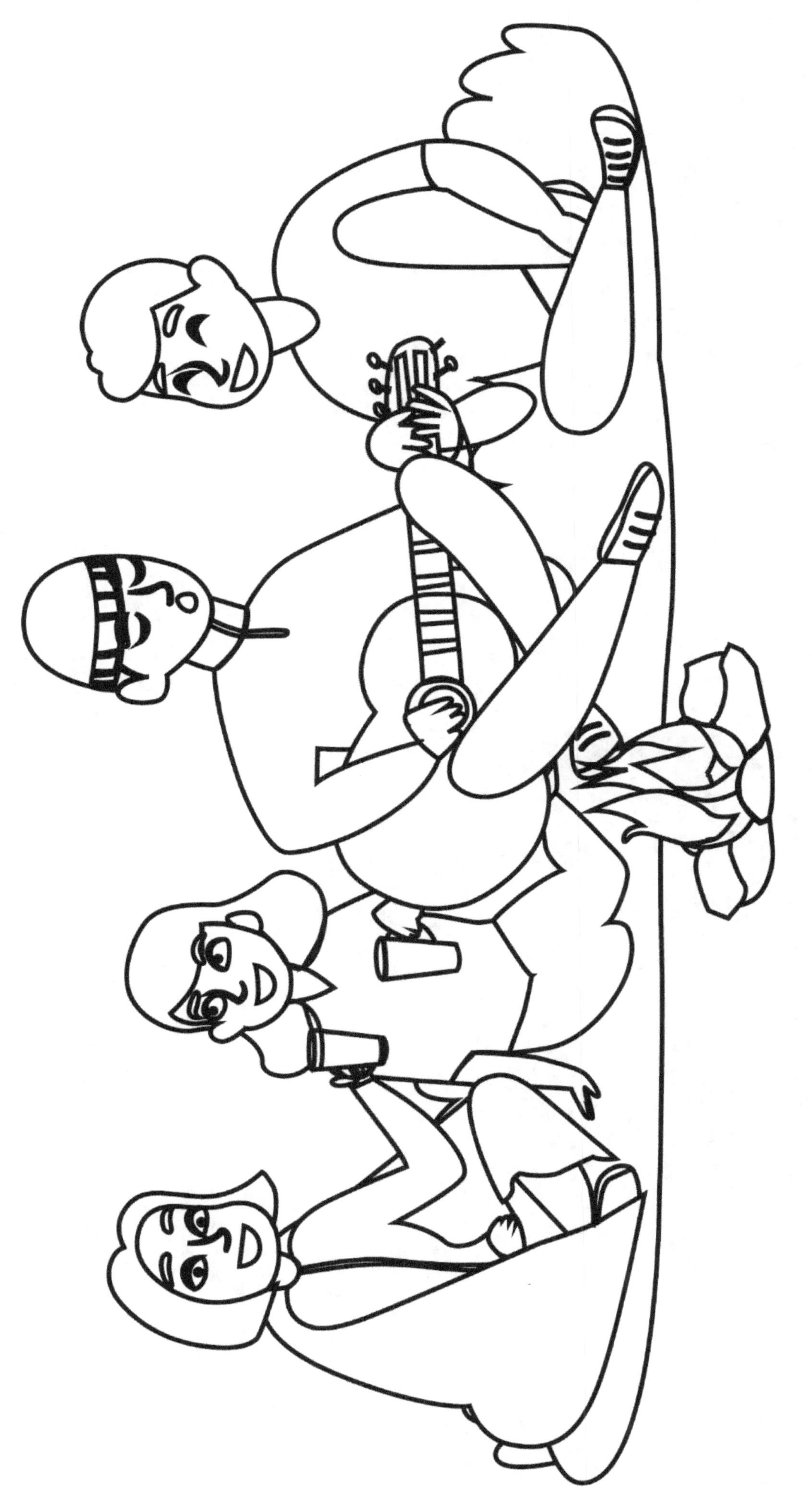

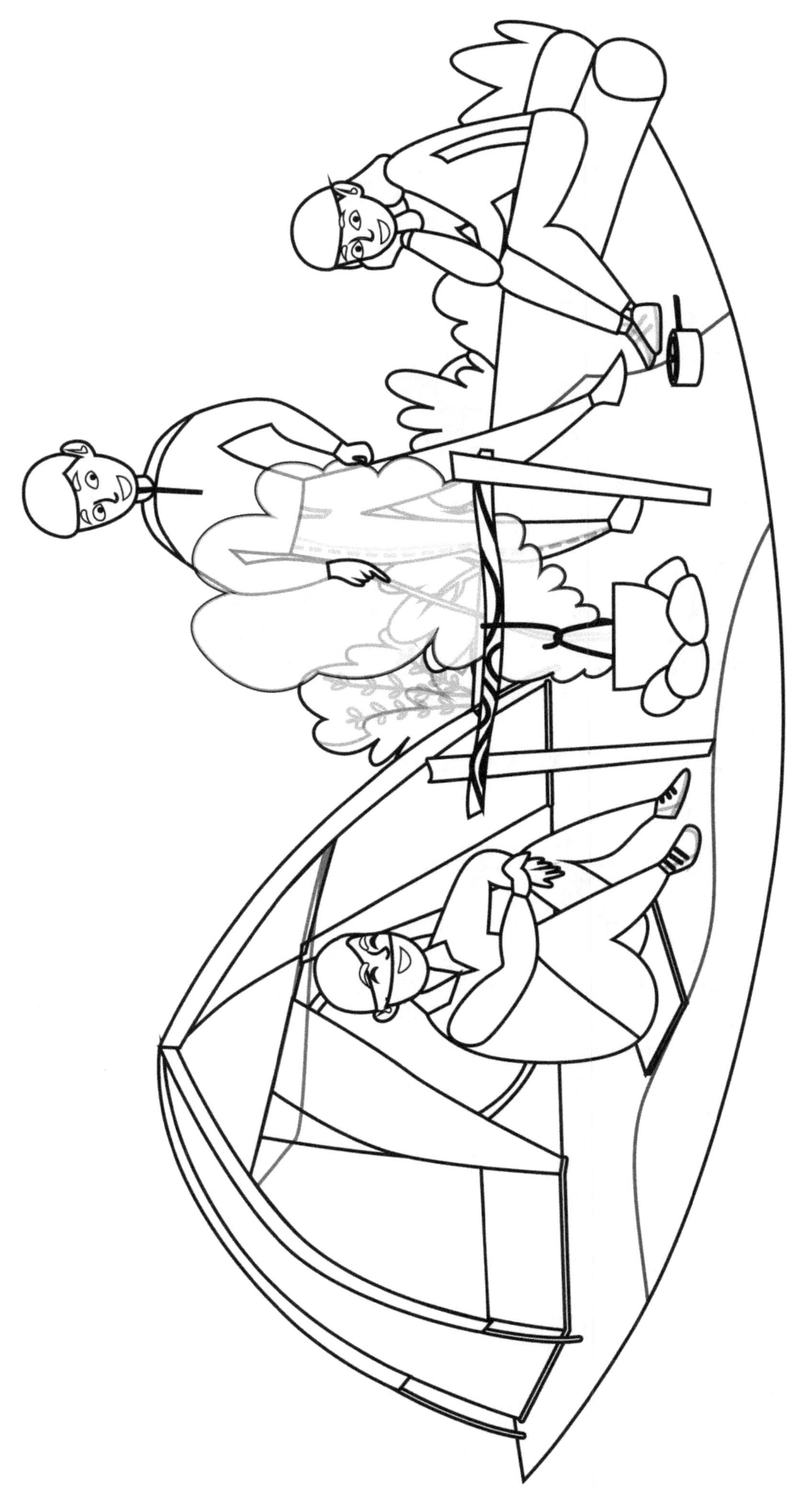

WHAT TO TAKE?

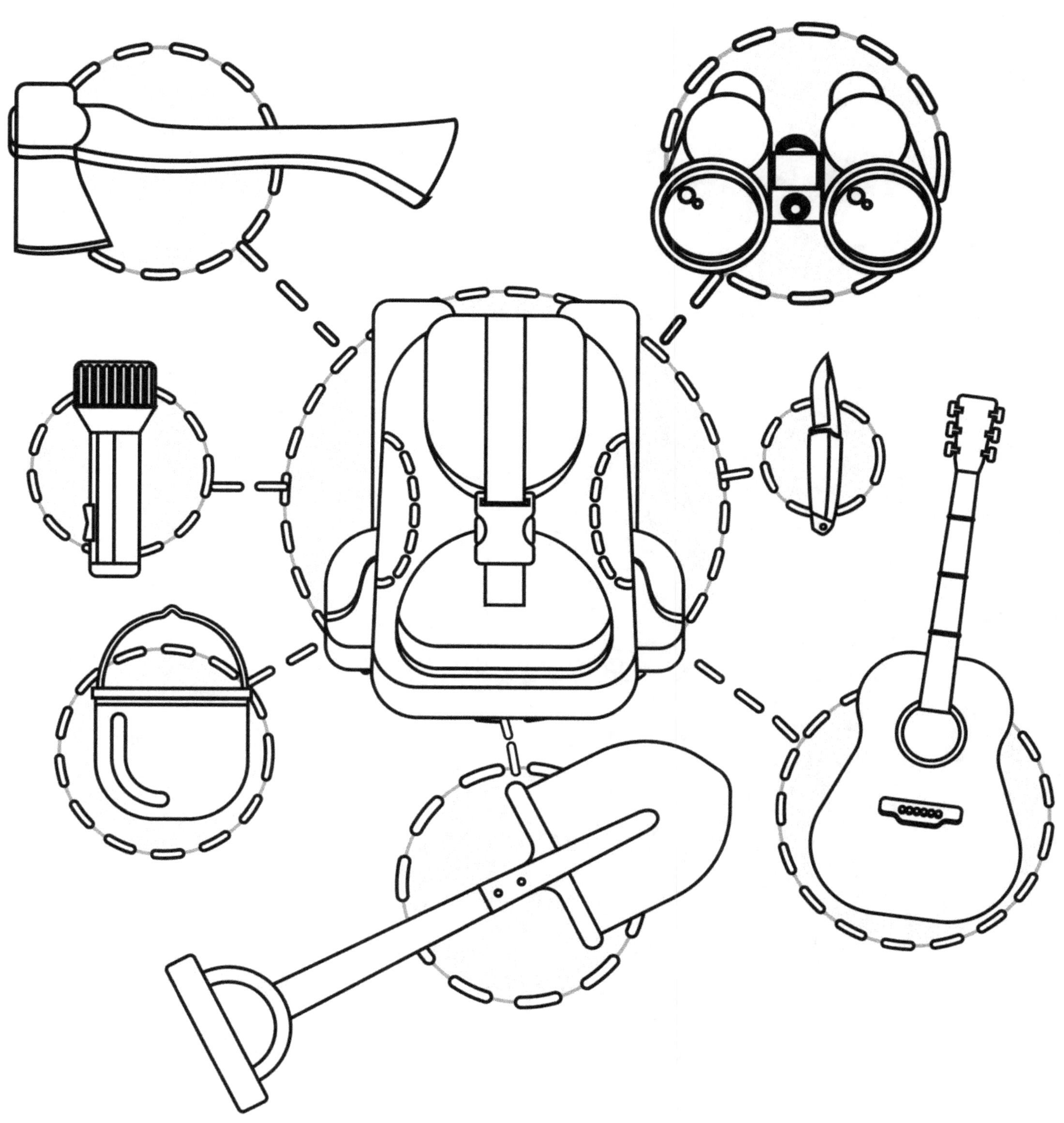

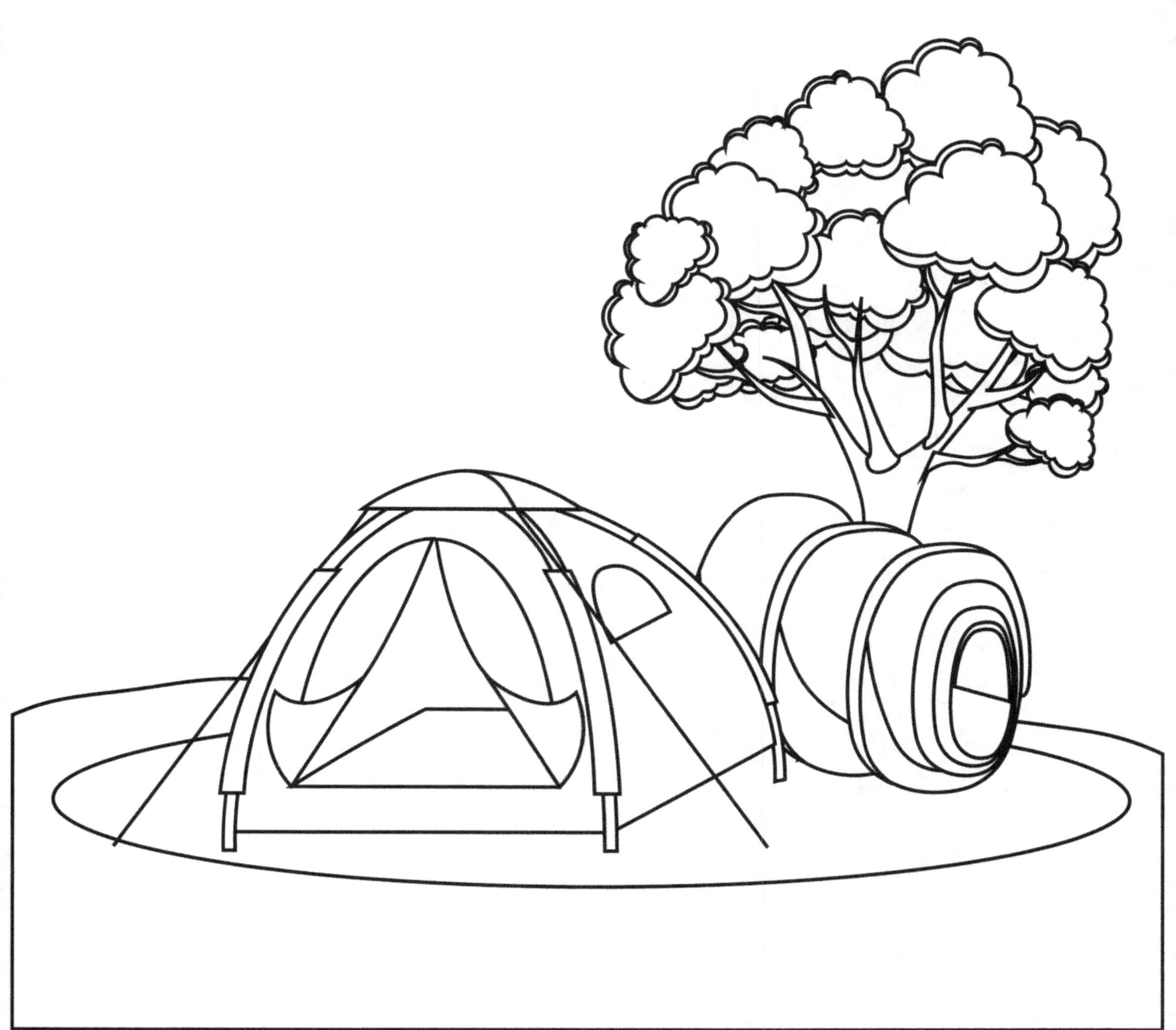

CAMPING

— WILD LIFE —

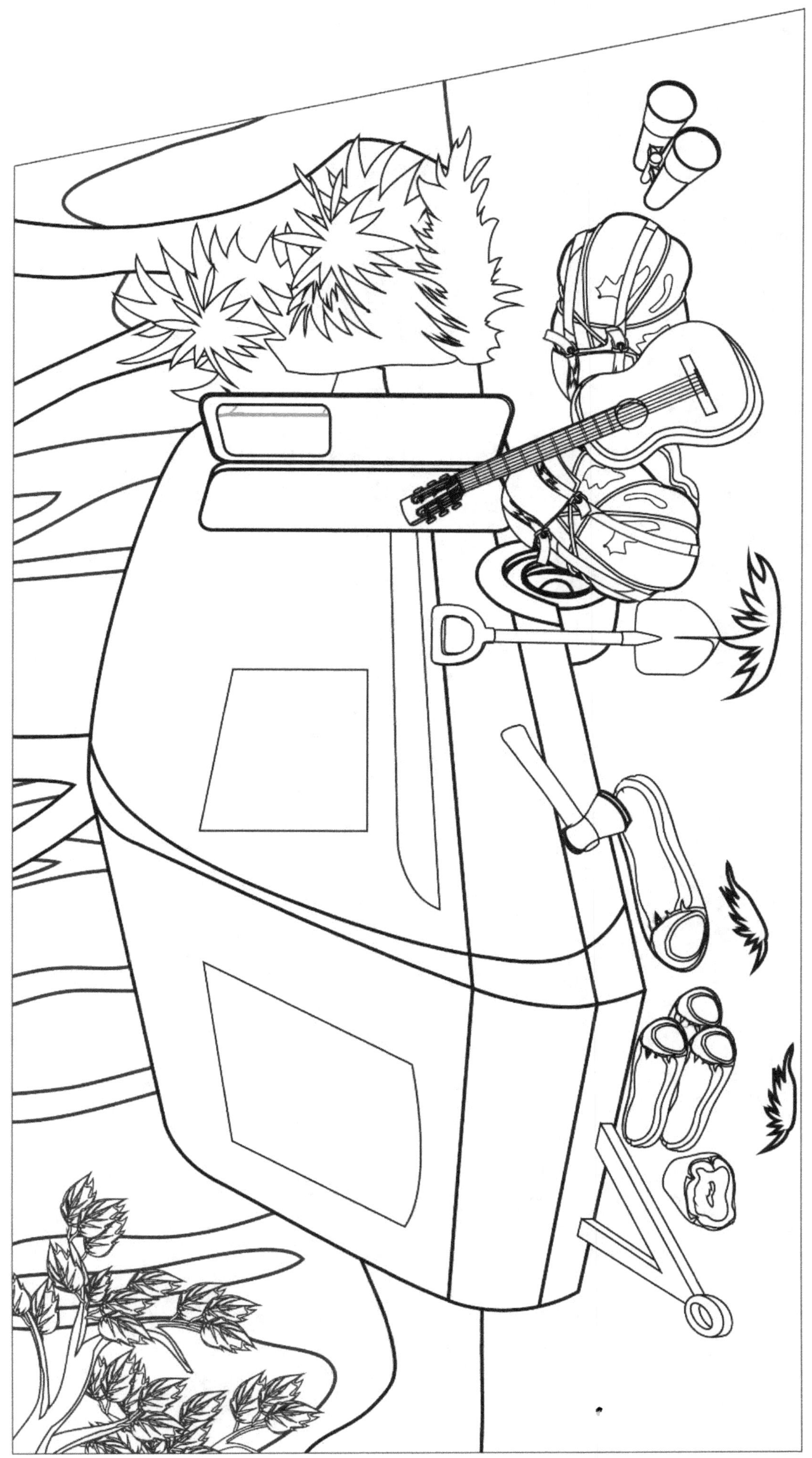

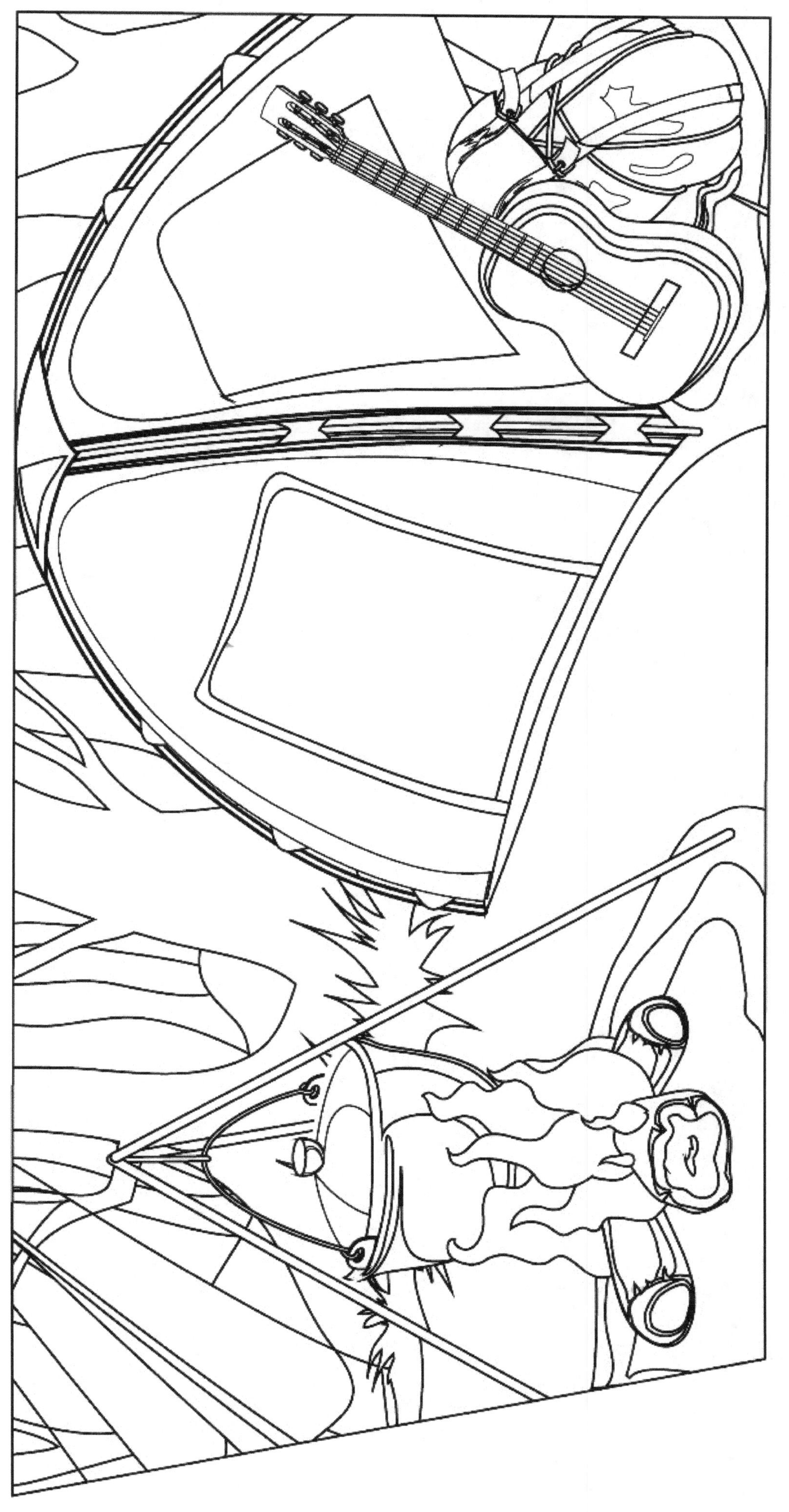

FOREST
CAMPING
OUTDOOR

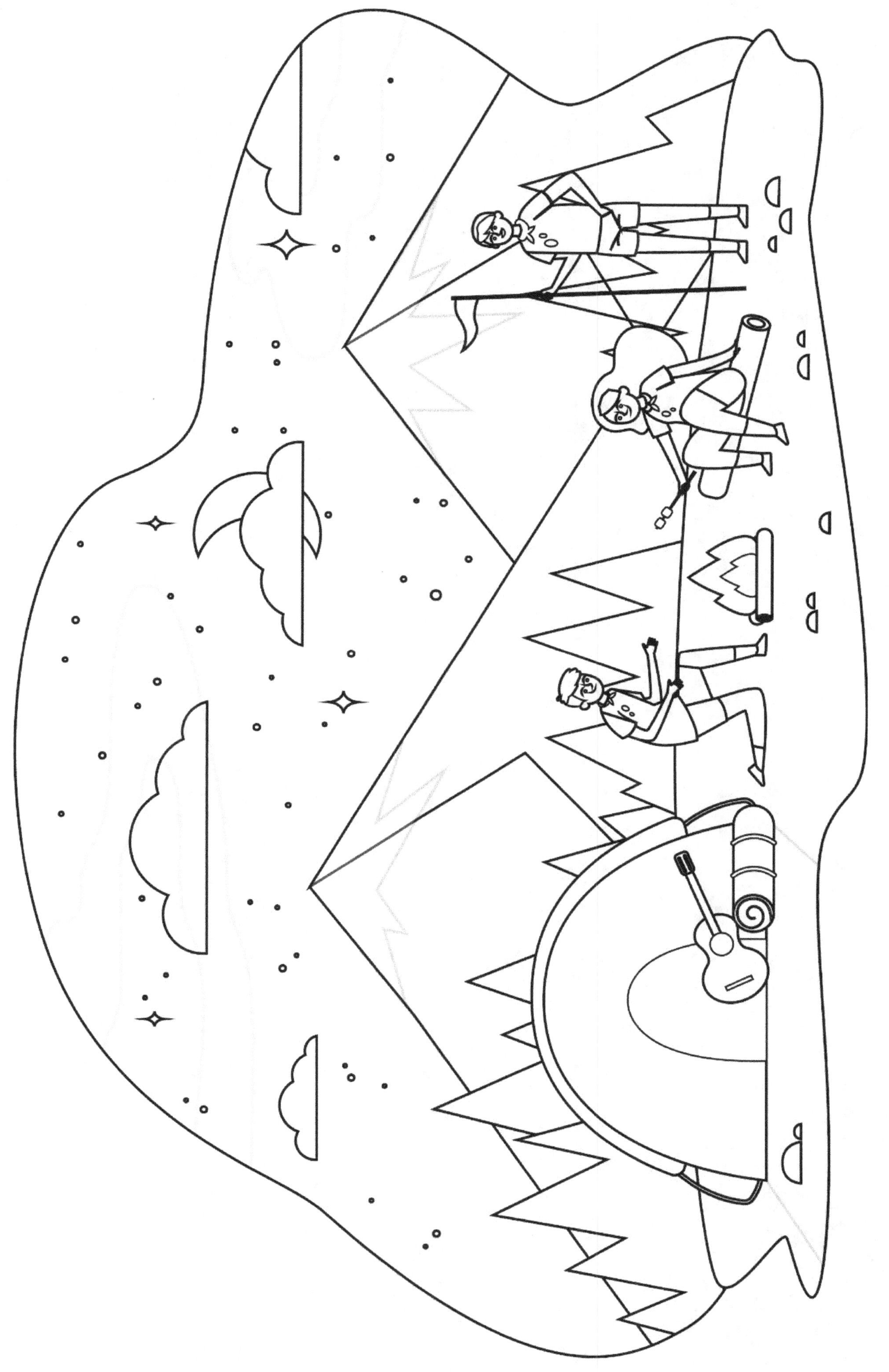

I ♥ Camping